Kamali Academy

AFRIKAN-CENTERED GRAMMAR WORKBOOK
FOR MIDDLE GRADES

Samori Camara, PhD

To Noliwe Mali-Sukari Camara

TABLE OF CONTENTS:

What Is A Sentence?

> A sentence is a group of words that expresses a complete thought.

The subject of the sentence tells whom or what the sentence is about. The predicate tells what the subject is or does. As long as a sentence contains both of these parts, it may be as brief as two words. Adding more information to the subject or predicate expands the sentence and makes it interesting. Remember to begin a sentence with a capital letter and end it with a punctuation mark.

Incomplete Sentence: The African continent.
Complete Sentence: The African continent is the second largest.
Subject: *The warriors* fought.   **Predicate:** A lion *lives in a pride.*

Try It!   Draw one line under each subject and two lines under each predicate.

1. African people originated in Africa.

2. The Nile River flows south to north.

3. The largest desert in the world is the Sahara Desert.

4. Scientists found the oldest human remains in Africa.

5. Africans created the first calendar.

6. Our African ancestors valued nature highly.

7. The living, dead, and unborn were respected.

8. The Dogon people of Mali discovered Sirius B.

9. A tree without roots cannot stand.

10. The oral tradition transmitted culture.

Write It!   What do you think of when you think of Africa? Write a description of your thoughts. When you read it over, check to see that you have used complete sentences.

Statements and Questions

> Two of the four kinds of sentences are called **declarative** and **interrogative.**

Both kinds of sentences begin with a capital letter and end with a punctuation mark. You can give variety and emphasis to your writing by using different kinds of sentences. A declarative sentence makes a statement and ends with a period (.). An interrogative sentence asks a question and ends with a question mark (?).

Declarative: Malcolm X was born Omaha, Nebraska.
Interrogative: What was Malcolm's birth name?

Try It!   Label each sentence as **declarative** or **interrogative**. Write the correct end punctuation for each sentence.

1. El-hajj Malik El-Shabazz was born Malcolm Little   _____

2. Elijah Muhammad taught Malcolm X   _____

3. When was Malcolm born   _____

4. Did Malcolm visit Africa   _____

5. Earl Little, his father, followed Marcus Garvey   _____

6. Malcolm married Betty Shabazz   _____

7. Do you like Malcolm   _____

8. What was Malcolm's dream job as a child   _____

9. Malcolm fought for the liberation of African people   _____

10. Are you as brave as this warrior   _____

Write It!   Which is your favorite Malcolm X quote? Write a poem that describes the meaning of the quote. Be sure to include both statements and questions?

Commands and Exclamations

> Two other kinds of sentences are called **imperative**, or **command**, sentences and **exclamatory** sentences.

An *imperative sentence* orders or asks someone to do something and ends with a period (.). An *exclamatory sentence* expresses strong emotion and ends with an exclamation mark (!). These two types of sentences can add weight to your idea and create excitement in your writing.

> **Imperative Sentence:** Do not let our flag touch the ground.
> **Exclamatory Sentence:** Let's write a song about Garvey!

Try It!   Label each sentence as *imperative* or *exclamatory*. Add the correct end punctuation to each sentence.

1.   Go to the library and study the Black Star Line   _____

2.   All students must read for one hour each day   _____

3.   What a great leader Marcus Garvey was   _____

4.   Observe the past to understand the present   _____

5.   Create solutions to the problems you see everyday   _____

6.   See the greatness within yourself   _____

7.   Do not allow fear to stop you   _____

8.   Imagine a world and create it   _____

9.   Dedicate your life to what you believe in   _____

10. Become even greater than our ancestors   _____

Write It!   Marcus Garvey had a vision and did the work to make it a reality. Think of one problem in your community and create a ten-part solution. You have a definite opinion about this, so use imperative and exclamatory sentences. Read it aloud to your class.

Complete Thoughts and Fragments

> To express a complete thought, a sentence needs a **subject** and a **predicate**.

Some groups of words look like sentences but are actually incomplete sentences known as **fragments**. A fragment does not express a complete thought. True sentences contain both a subject and a predicate.

Sentences: Tutankhamen was a boy king. He was not buried inside of a pyramid.

Fragments: Many riches inside. The curse of King Tut's grave.

Try It!   Label each group of words sentence or fragment. On a separate sheet of paper, add words to each fragment to make a complete sentence.

1.   Kemet is the original name of Egypt.   _____

2.   Egypt in is Africa.   _____

3.   Is also where the Nile River is located.   _____

4.   Imhotep designed the first pyramid.   _____

5.   Called the Saqqara step pyramid.   _____

6.   Hatshepsut was a female pharaoh.   _____

7.   Expanded foreign trade.   _____

8.   Khufu's pyramid is made of 2,300,000 stones.   _____

9.   Were great thinkers and builders.   _____

10.   Africans founded the first university.   _____

Write It!   Ancient Egyptians were great inventors. If you could invent anything, what would you create? Write about your invention, what it does, and how it works. Draw a picture to go along with it and share with your class or a family member. Ask your reader to find any fragments you may have forgotten to complete.

Complete Thoughts and Run-ons

> A **run-on sentence** joins together two sentences that should stand alone.

When you're writing quickly, you may put more into a sentence than it can hold. In that case, you have a **run-on sentence**. You can correct a run-on sentence by splitting it into two separate sentences. You can also correct a run-on by joining the two parts with a **comma** and **and**, **or**, or **but**.

Run-on sentence: Dr. Claud Anderson teaches us that we must have our own businesses you could help build your community.

Corrected sentence: Dr. Claud Anderson teaches us that we must have our won businesses. You could help build you community.

Try It!   Correct these run-on sentences, either by separating them into two sentences or by adding a comma and a conjunction.

1.   In the early 1900s, the Greenwood District of Tulsa, OK was known as Black Wall Street.

2.   Black people owned everything in their community it was a beautiful sight.

3.   The focal point of the community was the intersection of Greenwood and Archer.

4.   They had their own schools and hospital.

5.   Black restaurants were everywhere theaters and grocery stores too.

6.   In May 1921, a race riot destroyed Black Wall Street.

7.   Whites hated the success that Black people were having.

8.   They claimed a young Black boy assaulted a white girl in an elevator.

9.   The people of Black Wall Street fought back they refused to be bullied.

10.   We must recreate Black Wall Street wherever we are build businesses that serve us.

Write It!   Count the number of Black businesses in your community. Are there enough? Too many? Either way, write a paragraph about why you think that is and what you will do about it.

Simple and Complete Subjects

> The **complete subject** of a sentence contains all the words that tell whom or what the sentence is about.

Get to know the subject: study the examples below.

Simple Subject: *Rebellions* happened often.
Complete Subject: *Those fighters* had great courage.

Notice that the simple subject may also be the same as the complete subject.

Try It!   Draw two lines under the simple subject and one line under the complete subject.

1. Europeans kidnapped Turner's mother from Africa.
2. Nat Turner grew up on a plantation in Virginia.
3. The young boy learned to read at an early age.
4. Turner accepted Christianity and became a preacher.
5. A harsh overseer forced Turner to run away.
6. He experienced visions while in the woods.
7. An eclipse in February of 1831 prompted Turner to begin a rebellion.
8. The revolt lasted three days.
9. Turner and company killed fifty-seven whites.
10. The uprising intensified the anti-slavery movement.

Write It!   What do you think are the most important traits of a leader? Write a description of your favorite leader. When you have finished, circle the simple subject in each sentence. Underline the complete subject.

Compound Sentences

> A **compound sentence** contains two sentences joined by a comma and *and*, *or*, or *but*.

Forming compound sentences allows you to combine sentences that express similar ideas. Each sentence in the compound sentence has its own subject and predicate.

> Akili likes to play slow. Sanaa likes to play fast.
> Akili likes to play slow, but Sanaa likes to play fast.

> The Queen can move diagonally. It can move side-to-side.
> The Queen can move diagonally, and it can move side-to-side.

Try It!   Form a compound sentence from each pair of sentences. Remember to use a comma and *and*, *or*, or *but*.

1. We played chess today. I learned a lot.

2. It is a fun game. You must think hard.

3. I learned that the game comes from Africa. I was not surprised though.

4. To win you must think many moves ahead. It is over when you checkmate the King.

5. Games can be quick. Games can last hours.

6. The board has 64 squares. At the beginning of a match, there are 32 pieces.

7. My favorite piece could be the Queen. My favorite piece could be the rook.

8. The pawns only move forward. They attack diagonally.

9. You can play as black. You can play as white.

10. Chess improves concentration. It enhances critical thinking.

Write It!   What is your favorite game to play? Why do you like it? Write a short story about your favorite moment playing that game.

Combining Sentences: Compound Subjects and Predicates

> Two sentences that have the same subject or predicate may be combined into a single sentence.

Using compound subjects and compound predicates is a way to combine sentences and make your writing flow. A sentence may have both a compound subject and a compound predicate. You can combine some of your sentences in the following way:

Combining Subjects:
Amilcar led a revolt. I led a revolt, too.
Amilcar and I led revolts.

Combining Predicates:
Wangari fought for women. She planted trees.
Wangari fought for women and planted trees.

Try It!   On a separate sheet of paper, combine each compound subject or predicate using *and* or *or*. Underline the word that joins the parts of the compound.

1. Kunta Kinte never lost his culture. He fought to the end.

2. *Sankofa* was interesting. It was exciting too.

3. Lumumba watched the movie. I watched it, too.

4. *NightJohn* is about slavery. *Roots* is about slavery.

5. African movies move you. African movies inspire you.

6. Students should study our movies. Students should learn from our movies.

7. We support movies that support our best. We watch movies that show our best.

8. Documentaries are informational. Documentaries are great.

9. *The Spook Who Sat by the Door* is a great movie. *The Warrior Queen* is as well.

10. Jamal finished making his movie. I finished mine, too.

Write It!   What is your favorite movie about the Black experience? Write a brief summary of the movie and your thoughts about it. Be sure to use compound subjects and predicates when you can.

Combining Sentences: Compound Sentences

You can combine sentences that have related ideas using a comma and the word *and*, *or*, or *but*. Try combining sentences that have similar or related ideas. Your writing will be smoother, and the connections between your ideas will be easier to understand.

Combining Sentences:
Nia loves cookies. I love making them for her.
Nia loves cookies, and I enjoy making them for her.

Try It! Combine each pair of sentences using a comma and *and*, *or*, or *but*.

1. Marriage is not simply about the individuals. Marriage is not only about love.

2. African men and women must come together. They must love each other.

3. Black families must be whole. We will continue to lose if they are not.

4. We can live alone. Living together will make us stronger.

5. African men protect their families. African men provide financial and emotional stability.

6. A relationship is about two souls coming together. It is about bringing two purposes together.

7. Words are important. Actions mean more.

8. Marry someone with a similar vision. Be sure to support each other.

9. Relationships grow with attention, commitment, and investment. Without these things, they die.

10. Teach a man and you teach an individual. Teach a woman and you teach a nation.

Write It! What would be your relationship advice to your 25 year-old self? What should you do and not do?

What is a Noun?

> A **noun** names a person, place, thing, or idea.

Nouns are the naming words that you use in your writing. These who and what words are everywhere. A noun can be one or more words used together.

I like some *cartoons*. There is one *show* I really enjoy.
The *characters* inspire me. I can't wait until the next *episode*.

Try It!   Draw a line under each noun in the sentence.

1. Some cartoons are excellent.

2. *Black Panther* is my favorite.

3. T'chala is the main character.

4. The cartoon happens in Wakanda.

5. After the assassination of his father, T'chala searches for his killer.

6. Black Panther fights Captain America and wins.

7. His black suit and shield makes him look cool.

8. Black heroes are rare on television.

9. The word hero comes from Heru.

10. T'chala followed in the footsteps of his father.

Write It!   What is your favorite cartoon? What kind of lessons did you learn from it? Write a paragraph about that cartoon.

Common Nouns

A **common noun** names any person, place, thing, or idea.

Common nouns can refer to any of a group, without naming particular individuals. Concrete nouns are words such as *woman*, *horse*, and *saddle*. Abstract nouns include idea words like *patience*, *freedom*, and *silence*.

> We don't use our *eyes* to taste *soup*.
> Even if the *prison* is beautiful, you don't stay there at *peace*.

Try It!   To each blank, add a common noun that completes the sentence.

1. A _____ without roots cannot stand.

2. A roaring lion kills no _____.

3. Smooth _____ don't make a skillful sailor.

4. _____ is not yet rain.

5. He who wants _____ must brave the bees.

6. It takes a _____ to raise a child.

7. Family is an _____.

8. You eat an _____ one bite at a time.

9. Two _____ are better than one.

10. A watched _____ does not boil.

Write It!   Do you have a favorite proverb? Find and list five of your favorite proverbs. Be sure to memorize them.

Forming Plurals with S and ES

> * Form the plural of most nouns by adding *s*.
> * To nouns that end in *s*, *x*, *ch*, *zz*, or *sh*, add *es*.

Many nouns in the English language form the plural with the ending *s* or *es*. Check the ending of the singular noun before you make it plural in your writing.

The serious scholar   The serious scholars
The large bus   The large buses
The branch of the tree   The branches of the tree

Try It!   To each blank, add a common noun that completes the sentence.

1. An Adinkra <u>symbol</u> carries great meaning.   _____

2. You can find them on a <u>bench</u> or a fence.   _____

3. A <u>proverb</u> accompanies every symbol.   _____

4. I have a <u>shirt</u> with many Adinkra symbols.   _____

5. Learn about Adinkra at <u>lunch</u> today.   _____

6. Adinkra symbols come from the <u>country</u> of Ghana.   _____

7. The first <u>president</u> was Kwame Nkrumah.   _____

8. The <u>bus</u> can take you to his center.   _____

9. Find a <u>book</u> of African art.   _____

10. The Sankofa <u>bird</u> is famous.   _____

Write It!   Find an Adinkra symbol that moves you and write a short story that illustrates its meaning. Read it to a friend.

Singular and Plural Nouns

> A **singular noun** names one person, place, thing, or idea.

A **plural noun** names more than one person, place, thing, or idea. Knowing the rules for forming plural nouns is part of the writer's craft.

Add *s* to form the plural of most nouns.
  mask/masks   costume/costumes

Add *es* to form the plurals of nouns that end in *s, ss, x, ch,* or *sh.*
  rebus/rebuses   dress/dresses   box/boxes   patch/patches

Add *s* to form the plural of a noun that ends with a vowel and y.
  boy/boys   day/days   delay/delays   toy/toys

Change the *y* to *i* and add *es* to form the plural of a noun that ends with a consonant and y.
  party/parties   county/counties   jury/juries   story/stories

Try It!   Draw a line under the singular nouns in each sentence. Then write the plural form of each noun.

1. The soldier must know his enemy.   _____

2. The day will last long.   _____

3. The battle was won quickly.   _____

4. A match lit the fire.   _____

5. The party lasted until daybreak.   _____

6. The story teaches great lessons.   _____

7. Family is an army.   _____

8. The boy declared his alliance.   _____

9. The box was filled to the brim.   _____

10. The warrior keeps his cool.   _____

Write It!   What do you think the Afrikan proverb, "a warrior without war will war against self" mean? Write your answer and give examples. Make sure you've used plural nouns correctly.

Proper Nouns

- A proper noun names a particular person, place, thing, or idea.

- Proper nouns begin with a capital letter.

Using proper nouns where they are appropriate makes your writing specific and factual. Compare the sentences below.

That is a *place* on another *continent*.
Cameroon is a country in *Africa*.

We read the *book* and enjoyed the class.
We read *Two Thousand Seasons* and enjoyed the class.

Try It!   Draw a line under each common noun. Draw two lines under each proper noun.

1. Patrice Lumumba served as Prime Minister of the Congo.

2. Officials deported Marcus Garvey from the port of New Orleans.

3. Booker T. Washington, a leader, founded Tuskegee University.

4. In 1964, Malcolm X took a pilgrimage to Mecca.

5. Ida Be Wells exposed lynchings across the United States.

6. Born in Omaha, Nebraska, Malcolm's family soon moved to another state.

7. The Kwame Nkrumah Center in Ghana inspired me.

8. We should all be leaders like Yaa Asantewaa.

9. Egypt was originally called Kemet.

10. Fannie Lou Hamer led students and activists in Mississippi during the Civil Rights Movement.

Write It!   Where would you like to go? Who would you like to meet? Write a journal entry about three places you'd like to go and three people you'd like to meet.

Forming Plurals with IES and EYS

> - To form the plural of a noun that ends with a consonant and *y*, change the *y* to *i* and add *es*.
> - To form the plural of a noun that ends in *ey*, add *s*.

Learn the rules for forming plurals with these endings, and keep your writing clear and correct.

> The *nanny* watched the children. The *nannies* are here.
> The *valley* is low. The *valleys* have flowers.

Try It!   Change the underlined singular noun in each sentence to a plural noun.

1. The <u>history</u> of our people is great and extensive.   _____

2. In African culture, a <u>baby</u> is given a name on the 8th day after birth. _____

3. A <u>valley</u> allows you to appreciate the peak.   _____

4. Your <u>body</u> is your temple.   _____

5. A man without a <u>lady</u> is empty.   _____

6. My <u>daddy</u> provides a great example of manhood.   _____

7. Your <u>story</u> can inspire millions. Tell it.   _____

8. The <u>study</u> shows that African-centered education is the key.   _____

9. We drove down the dark <u>alley</u> quickly.   _____

10. Our herbs in the plant <u>nursery</u> are growing well.   _____

Write It!   What is an inspiring story you have heard? Why did story inspire you? Write a journal entry recounting that story and how it inspires you today.

Forming The Possessive of Singular Nouns

> • Form the possessive of a singular noun by adding an apostrophe (') and s ('s) to the noun.

A noun that shows possession, or ownership, is called a possessive noun. You can use possessive nouns in your writing to make it concise and avoid repeating the phrase "of the." Notice that the 's stands for the phrase "of the."

the love of the woman   the woman's love
a day of rain   a day's rain   the rays of the sun   the sun's rays

Try It!   On a separate sheet of paper, rewrite each sentence by replacing the word in parentheses with an apostrophe and a singular possessive noun.

1. Without (the work of the farmer), many of us would not eat.

2. Agriculture is not just (the domain of men).

3. Farmers know that it is (the roots of the plant) that keep it stable.

4. (The rays of the sun) nurture the plants.

5. (The rain of the cloud) soak the ground so plants can drink.

6. We love (the fruits of nature).

7. (The potential of the seed) is at its core.

8. (The growth of each flower) ensures our future.

9. (The freshness of homegrown food) makes the work worth it.

10. (The work of the gardener) is never done.

Write It!   Can you imagine a plant that refused to grow? Write a short story from the perspective of a seed that refuses to grow and blossom. Then write one about a seed that knew growth was natural. Be sure to use possessive nouns in your work.

Compound Words

> • A **compound word** is made from two or more words joined together.

A compound is called **open** when the words in it are written separately. When a compound is written as one word, it is called a **closed compound**. Expand your vocabulary, and use compound words in your writing.

uplift   homemade   table talk   fruit cup

Try It!   Underline the compound word in each sentence.

1. A thunderstorm failed to stop Afrikans from escaping.

2. "Any place is better than the plantation," Malcolm said.

3. Women and men shared leadership in maroon communities.

4. Do your homework on Queen Nandi of the maroons.

5. Moonlight led Afrikans to freedom.

6. By the campfire, they told stories of liberation.

7. Maroons grew their own food and raised livestock.

8. They protected themselves with firearms and other weapons.

9. The maroon community was an outlet for enslaved Afrikans.

10. The maroons had a superhuman ability to preserve Afrikan culture.

Write It!   If you could create your own community, what would you include? What institutions? Rituals? Laws? Write a newspaper article explaining the elements of your new community.

Action Verbs

> • An **action verb** expresses action. Action verbs show what the subject does or did.

Verbs can express both actions that you can see and those that you can't. Include both types in your writing, and watch your sentences come alive!

The baby *sings* her baba's name.   The mama *feeds* her child.

The author *writes* well.   We *read* her book.

Try It!   Complete each sentence with an action verb.

1. Yaa Asantewaa _____ her people.

2. We _____ the Black National Anthem.

3. The revolutionary _____ into battle.

4. The Golden Stool _____ with the Ashanti people.

5. Europeans _____ Afrika during colonialism.

6. We _____ several Afrikan languages.

7. The chief _____ with his people.

8. The women _____ because the men would not step up.

9. Some warriors _____ until they won.

10. The village _____ when the stool returned.

Write It!   Write a pledge that every Afrikan student should recite in the morning. Be sure to include action verbs.

Main and Helping Verbs

> • The **main verb** shows what the subject is or does. The
> **helping verb** helps the main verb to show action in the
> sentence.

When you write, you use helping verbs as well as main verbs. The chart of common helping verbs below will help you to show where the action is.

am	are	were	shall	has	can
is	was	will	have	had	could

We *are progressing* towards liberation.
My home *could use* some Afrikan art.

Try It!   Draw one line under the helping verb. Draw two lines under the main verb.

1. The Sit-in Movement was led by college students.

2. These students could endure taunts and harassment.

3. A meeting was held in Raleigh, North Carolina.

4. At the meeting, they would start S.N.C.C..

5. The activists were discussing how to continue the fight.

6. Ella Baker was key to the group's development.

7. Stokely Carmichael was elected chairman in 1966.

8. Carmichael had began speaking about Black Power, not non-violence.

9. The organization would stop focusing of voting rights.

10. S.N.C.C. has left a great legacy that we should learn about.

Write It!   Have you ever started an organization or wanted to start one? What would the organization be about? Write a paragraph about the organization's philosophy.

Linking Vers

> • A **linking verb** connects the subject of the sentence to a noun or adjective in the predicate.

A verb that does no show action is called a linking verb. Many linking verbs are forms of the verb *to be*. Many of your sentences contain linking verbs. Notice that some verbs may serve either as linking verbs or as action verbs.

The hibiscus tea smells delicious. Let me smell it, too.

Some other linking verbs are *am, is, are, was, were, will be, seem, appear, look, taste*, and *feel*.

Try It!   Underline the linking verb in each sentence.

1. Afrikan clothes are fashionable.

2. They seem exotic to some.

3. In some places, Afrikan clothes were the norm.

4. Dashikis look good on Black men.

5. I feel beautiful in my Afrikan garb.

6. People in ethnic clothes appear regal.

7. Natural hair and Afrikan clothes are lovely.

8. I am eager to wear my own clothes.

9. Supporting European designers is foolish.

10. One day, we will all wear Afrikan clothes.

Write It!   Could you create a clothing line for Black people? What would it be called? What kind of clothes would it be? Formal, casual, t-shirts, etc.? Write a paragraph about you new clothing line.

Present-Tense Verbs

- A verb shows when an action happens through its **tense**. **Present-tense verbs** show action that is happening now.

Knowing how to form verb tenses will help your writing to tell time punctually. Here are some rules for forming the present tense.

For most verbs, add *s*: run/runs, walk/walks, jump/jumps.

For verbs ending *in s, ch, sh, x,* and *z,* add *es.*

Press/presses   match/matches   push/pushes   mix/mixes   buzz/buzzes

For verbs ending with a consonant and *y,* change y to *i* and add *es.*

Try It!   Add the correct present-tense ending to the main form of the verb in parentheses.

1. Noliwe (love) her community.   _____

2. She (give) her talents whenever she can.   _____

3. Her baba (teach) Noliwe her history.   _____

4. Sometimes her baba (push) her to study harder. _____

5. He (encourage) Noliwe every step of the way.   _____

6. Noliwe (read) very well.   _____

7. Today, her baba (continue) to challenge her.   _____

8. With his help, Noliwe (grow) into a great leader. _____

9. Her baba (buzz) with pride.   _____

10. Noliwe (relax) by playing chess.   _____

Write It!   When you have a child, what would you name them? Would it be an Afrikan name? Write a letter to your future child. Tell them their name, what it means, and why you chose it.

Past-Tense Verbs

> • **Past-tense verbs** show action that has already happened.

Past-tense verbs express action that is competed. In your writing, use the correct endings to tell that events took place in the past. Here are some handy rules:

For most verbs, add *ed*:   load/loaded   pick/picked

For verbs that end with *e*, drop the *e* and add *ed*.   Free/freed

For verbs that end with a consonant and *y*, change the y to *i* and add *ed*.
Marry/married   study/studied   bury/buried

For verbs ending with a single vowel and a consonant, double the final consonant and add *ed*.   grip/gripped   tan/tanned

Try It!   Write the past tense of the verb in parentheses.

1. The Black Panther Party was (start) in 1966.   _____

2. Huey P. Newton and Bobby Seale (establish) the organization. _____

3. They quickly (develop) the Ten-Point Platform.   _____

4. It (state) their demands.   _____

5. The original members (study) Malcolm, Marx, and Mao.   _____

6. Because they (refuse) oppression, they (fight) the police. _____

7. The Panthers (feed) thousands with their Free Breakfast Program.   _____

8. COINTELPRO (murder) many of the members.   _____

9. We are still (inspire) by their powerful work.   _____

10. The Panthers (rise) up to fight and so will we.   _____

Write It!   Research Huey P. Newton and write a brief biographical sketch of his life. Be sure to use past-tense verbs.

Future-Tense Verbs

> • **Future-tense verbs** show that an action has not yet taken place. Add *shall* or *will* to the present tense of the verb to show its future tense.

What are you expecting? When you write about something that will happen, use the future tense to keep your meaning clear.

Abayomi *will unveil* her new painting. We *shall visit* her home tonight.

Try It!   Fill in the blank with the future tense of the verb in parentheses.

1. We _____ free in the future. (get)

2. Brothers and sisters _____ together. (come)

3. We don't need outside help. We _____ ourselves. (lead)

4. The ancestors and elders _____ help us along the way. (help)

5. The revolution _____ impossible. (seem)

6. But, we _____ in the end. (prevail)

7. Together we _____ . (win)

8. Liberation _____ when we embrace our culture. (begin)

9. Our culture _____ our movement. (strengthen)

10. We _____ what we will. (accomplish)

Write It!   What are you looking forward to doing? What are your goals for the future? Write a letter to yourself ten years from now explaining the things you will accomplish by that age.

Using The Verb *Be*

> - The verb *be* changes its form according to special rules in order to agree with its subject.

Refer to these examples for forming agreement with be, and your writing will be perfectly clear.

I am/was   you are/were   he, she, or it is/was
We are/were   they are/were

The spirit is with us. We are surrounded by ancestral wisdom.
The initiates were friendly at the lecture. I was not nervous in their presence.

Try It!   Complete each sentence with the correct form of the verb *be*.

1. The Ausar Auset Society _____ started in 1973.

2. Ra Un Nefer Amen _____ the founder.

3. Their practices _____ based on Kemetic culture.

4. Our Kemetic ancestors _____ very spiritual people.

5. The philosophy of Ausar Auset _____ to awaken the god or goddess

within you.

6. Participants _____ given guidance by the Oracle.

7. Nutrition, family relationships, and vegetarian cooking _____

important to members.

8. Books _____ written by Amen to help initiates.

9. Ancient Kemet _____ a great African civilization.

10. Many of us _____ ignorant of African spiritual systems.

Write It!   Research three Afrikan spiritual systems and discuss their major ideas
including their names for the Creator.

Using The Verb *Do*

> • The verb *do* also forms agreement with subjects according to special rules.

Like *be*, the verb *do* has an irregular form. That means it is spelled differently depending on its subject. Use it well in your writing, and you will do readers a favor. Here are some examples of agreement with *do*.

I, you, we do/have done/did/had done

He, she, it does/has done/did/had done

They do/have done/did/had done

I *did* my best, but I *have done* better. You *do* a great job every time.

Try It!   Complete each sentence with the correct present or past-tense form of the verb *do*.

1. We _____ a Kwanzaa celebration every year.

2. The Afrikan-centered school _____ the history portion.

3. In the past, we _____ great programs.

4. We _____ seven programs last year.

5. The Akotos _____ the cooking for the events.

6. Sankofa Dancers _____ the dance portion.

7. Mama Suma will _____ the libation this year.

8. All the parents _____ learn the seven principles, if they

_____ not know them before.

9. I _____ a speech on life purpose two years ago.

10. We _____ great work.

Write It!   The big moment has arrived, and you are about to perform. Write a paragraph that tells of the preparation and actual moment of the event.

Using The Verb *Have*

> • The verb *have* is another irregular verb that forms agreement with subjects according to special rules.

Have you noticed how you use this verb in your writing? Take a look at the examples below so you will use this verb correctly.

I have/had   you have/had   he, she, it has/had
We have/had   they have/had

We have a surprise for you!   You had no idea about it.

It has some interesting traditions.   They have plenty of wisdom.

Try It!   In each sentence, underline the correct verb from the pair in parentheses.

1. We (has/have) lost many of our traditions.

2. Enslavement (has/have) broken our connection to the motherland.

3. Most of us (has/have) European names.

4. Some (has/have) an anti-African worldview.

5. You once (has/had) your own names and culture.

6. We (has/have) to reclaim our Africanness.

7. I (has/had) a dream that we would.

8. Do you (has/have) the courage to step back to tradition?

9. The future (has/have) great things in store if you do.

10. I (has/have) faith that we will find our way home.

Write It!   What is one thing that we practiced in the past and now have lost? Write a paragraph about what it was, the meaning, and how we can get it back.

Irregular Verbs *See, Go, Come,* and *Take*

> • **Irregular verbs** show the past tense by changing their spelling.

As you know, regular verbs take *ed* endings to show past tense. When you write using irregular verbs, you need to be aware of their special past-tense forms. *See, go, come,* and *take* are all irregular verbs. Notice how their spelling changes.

see/saw/has, have, had seen   come/came/has, have, had come

go/went/has, have, had gone   take/took/has, have, had taken

Try It!   Write the correct past-tense form of the verb in parentheses.

1. Marcus Garvey (come) to town.   _____

2. Our whole family (go) to community center.   _____

3. We (see) him clearly from our seats.   _____

4. My uncle (take) pictures of him.   _____

5. I (go) through a lot of trouble to read his speeches before he came. _____

6. That day, I (take) the oath to be apart of the U.N.I.A.   _____

7. After that, we (see) him every time he (come) to town.   _____

8. My cousin Sankara (come) to the center too.   _____

9. Garvey never (go) to Africa.   _____

10. I am glad I (see) such a great leader.   _____

Write It!   Did you ever see anyone who really grabbed your attention? Write a news article about this occasion. It's all right to make it fiction, so you can exercise either your memory or your imagination.

Irregular Verbs *Write, Sing, Bring,* and *Say*

> • The **Irregular verbs** *write, sing, bring,* and *say* also show the past tense through changes in their spelling.

This group of verbs is **irregular**, so you should get familiar with the way they look in the past tense. You'll use them often in your writing.

write/wrote/has, have, had written
bring/brought/has, have, had brought
sing/sang/has, have, had sung
say/said/has, have, had said

The author said our poems were excellent.
Our parents have written notes of permission for the camping trip.

Try It!   Write the correct past-tense form of the verb in parentheses.

1. James Weldon Johnson _____ the Black National Anthem.

2. We _____ that song everyday at school.

3. The song _____ me to tears one time.

4. My baba _____ , "Put your fist up when you sing it."

5. After the song, we _____ the African pledge.

6. "Lift Every Voice and Sing" must be _____ with passion and pride.

7. "Sing a song full of the hope that the present has _____ us."

8. Yaa _____ a poem inspired by the song.

9. The poem _____ back memories.

10. The last line of the poem _____ , "Let us march on until victory is won."

Write It!   Read the Black National Anthem. What is your favorite verse? Why?

Subject-Verb Agreements: Singular

> • Add *s* or *es* to a present-tense verb when the subject is a singular noun or *he, she,* or *it*.

A verb agrees with its subject in number. A singular subject takes a singular verb. Since you use verbs in all of your writing, take some time to review them now. See the lesson Present-Tense Verbs for the rules.

The carnival begins in two days.

The dancer stretches his hamstrings before the parade.

Try It!   Complete each sentence with the correct present-tense form of the verb in parentheses.

1. Kofi (dance) to the rhythm of the African drum.   _____

2. Nzinga (move) her hips to the beat.   _____

3. The drummer (touch) the sides of his drum.   _____

4. A little boy (wish) he could play that well.   _____

5. An older dancer (stretch) before joining the circle.   _____

6. African dance (involve) spirit.   _____

7. It (connect) us to our ancestors.   _____

8. The spectator (look) on in amazement.   _____

9. The singer (sing) with power.   _____

10. Dance (heal) the soul.   _____

Write It!   You are a newspaper writer covering an African dance event. Write an article on the event that captures the excitement and energy. Use plenty of action verbs, and check their tenses.

Subject-Verb Agreements: Plural

> - Verbs agree with their subject in number. Do not add *s* or *es* to the present-tense verb when the subject is a plural noun or *I, you, we,* or *they*.

In your writing, you use both singular and plural nouns. Know how to make verbs agree with both forms, and your reader will be able to follow where you lead.

We *study* African languages at our school.

College students *teach* the course.

They *write* a lot on the chalkboard.

Try It!   In each sentence, underline the correct verb from the pair in parentheses.

1. The students (enjoy/enjoys) the Kiswahili class.

2. Their young instructors (bring/brings) enthusiasm to the subject.

3. Millions (speak/speaks) Kiswahili in east Africa.

4. Students (learn/learns) better when it is about their culture.

5. I (wants/wants) to learn that language too.

6. You (understand/understands) Kiswahili already, don't you?

7. The phrases (seem/seems) difficult, at first.

8. With practice, they (get/gets) easier.

9. Africans (work/works) hard to communicate with each other.

10. Kiswahili classes (teach/teaches) African culture as well.

Write It!   Is there a language or other skill that you would like to learn, or that you have already mastered? Write an editorial encouraging others to pursue this endeavor.

Contractions with Not

> - A verb combined with the word not is called a **verb contraction**. An **apostrophe** (') shows the letter or letters that have been left out of the contraction.

A contraction is a word made from two words. Contractions are used in informal writing, such as a friendly letter or a short story. They are never used in reports or business letters. Below are some verb contractions.

Should not/shouldn't   is not/isn't   was not/wasn't   do not/don't

Must not/mustn't   cold not/couldn't   have not/haven't   does not/doesn't

Try It!   Replace the underlined words with the correct contraction.

1.   I <u>cannot</u> listen to music that degrades Black people.   _____

2.   Kwame <u>does not</u> like Country songs.   _____

3.   Nzinga <u>could not</u> play the djembe drum the first time she tried. _____

4.   Biko <u>is not</u> a strong dancer.   _____

5.   Assata and Afeni <u>have not</u> heard the songs on the radio.   _____

6.   Fela Kuti <u>could not</u> sing meaningless lyrics.   _____

7.   Nile and Noble <u>do not</u> enjoy Otis Redding, for some reason.   _____

8.   Bob Marley <u>was not</u> the best, but he was close.   _____

9.   Dead Prez <u>has not</u> made a bad album.   _____

10.   We <u>should not</u> listen to trashy music.   _____

Write It!   We all have at least one type of music we love. What if you were stranded on a desert island? Name the five songs you would take with you and why.

What is an Adjective?

> • An **adjective** describes a noun or a pronoun. Adjectives are words that tell *what kind* or *how many*.

Make your writing colorful and exact with adjectives. You'll notice that these descriptive words often come before the noun or pronoun. Adjectives may also follow linking verbs.

We moved to a *wonderful* neighborhood. (what kind)

The new neighborhood has *several* revolutionary families. (how many)

Our old neighborhood was *cramped*. (after a linking verb)

Try It!   Draw a line under each adjective. Draw two lines under the noun the adjective describes.

1.   Zora Neale Hurston was a great writer.

2.   She was born on January 7, 1891, in a sleepy Alabama town.

3.   Hurston wrote several books about the Black experience in the South.

4.   Her work celebrated strong Black people, especially women.

5.   Hurston considered her blackness a wonderful gift.

6.   Few writers gained her popularity during the Harlem Renaissance.

7.   Zora said she was born in the all-black town of Eatonville, Florida.

8.   Her most famous work is *Their Eyes Were Watching God*.

9.   The story follows Janie through several Black communities and love relationships.

10.   Hurston was an outspoken critic of integration.

Write It!   Do you ever notice Black culture? Write a newspaper article describing Black culture to a friend from the continent of Africa.

Adjectives That tell *What Kind*

> • **Adjectives** that tell *what kind* describe what a person, place, or thing is like. Two or more adjectives before a noun are usually separated by commas.

When you want to tell readers how something or someone looks, acts, or seems, choose an adjective that tells what kind. Using precise adjectives lets readers share your experience.

Her smile was *majestic*. Her *white* teeth shone in the day.
Her *warm, generous* nature welcomed us. The *comfortable* home hear our conversations.

Try It!   Complete each sentence with adjectives that tell what kind.

1.   The _____ book lifted our spirits.

2.   Its _____ language made reading it simple.

3.   _____ , _____ thoughts filled our minds.

4.   _____ ideas gave way to basic principles.

5.   A _____ story stands out in my mind.

6.   The chapters were _____ .

7.   My eyes felt _____ after reading one passage.

8.   No pages went unread in this _____ book.

9.   The _____ author is one of our greatest teachers.

10.   Throughout the work, the information was _____ and

_____ .

Write It!   Do you have a favorite book? What is the title? Would you recommend it to your friends? Write a brief review of your favorite book. Be sure to use adjectives that tell what kind.

Adjectives That tell *How Many*

> • Some **adjectives** tell *how many* about a subject.

When one of the adjectives in a series tells *how many*, a comma is not needed. Adjectives give different kinds of information about number. These adjectives may express a **cardinal number**, such as *four or one hundred*. Adjectives also can be **ordinal numbers**, such a *first or third*. Adjectives such as *many* or *few* give more general information about number.

Try It!   Draw a line under each adjective that tells how many.

1.   Few people know about Ida B. Wells-Barnett.

2.   She documented hundreds of lynchings across the country.

3.   Several white hate groups wanted her dead.

4.   Some people called upon her to help them find justice.

5.   Ida was one of eight children.

6.   She attended Shaw University (now Rust College) for several years.

7.   Barnett wrote dozens of articles in response to injustice across the South.

8.   In her last years of life, Barnett wrote about the race riots of 1917, 1919, and 1922.

9.   Ida was one of the first women to fight lynching publicly.

10.   Many pictures of Barnett still exist. Look them up.

Write It!   Research lynching. Write a first-person account of a lynching from the perspective of Black people forced to watch a family member lynched.

Articles

> - An **article** is an adjective that describes a noun or another adjective. *A, an*, and *the* are articles.

You use these short but important words in many of your sentences. Remember to use *a* before a noun that beings with a consonant. Use *an* before a noun that begins with a vowel. Use *the* before either type of noun when you want to refer to one or more specific persons, places, or things.

The African-American History Museum is fun to visit. *A* new exhibit opens today.

An area for Kemet was placed in the museum.

Try It! Underline the correct article of each pair in parentheses.

1. (A, The) Black History Month observance started as Black History Week.

2. (A, An) man named Carter G. Woodson established the week in 1926.

3. He was (a, an) excellent scholar.

4. During the month, children have (a, an) opportunity to learn more about themselves.

5. However, (a, an) Black person should study themselves every day.

6. (A, An) month is nice, but Black History is 365 days a year.

7. Wonderful materials are available for (a, an) serious students of our culture.

8. (A, The) month can be used for good.

9. It's not simply (a, an) celebration of African food and dance.

10. We must use it to learn about (a, the) wisdom of our ancestors.

Write It! Describe your ideal Black History Month program. Write a proposal for your school or parents on how you what your next Black History Month to unfold.

Predicate Adjectives

> - A **predicate adjective** is a word that modifies or describes the subject. A predicate adjective follows a linking verb.

A predicate adjective gives more information about the subject of a sentence. In your writing, you use predicate adjectives after linking verbs such as *is, feels, appears, sounds, acts, grows, seems, tastes, remains, looks, and becomes.*

That puppy looks *hungry* even after his meal.

Try It!   Draw one line under the predicate adjective in each sentence. Draw two lines under the subject it modifies.

1.   The elder seems wise.

2.   The children appear comfortable.

3.   I bet that vegan gumbo is delicious.

4.   The people eating it look satisfied.

5.   The audience becomes quiet when the program starts.

6.   The speaker's information feels heavy.

7.   The drum beat sounds energetic.

8.   The crowd remains silent.

9.   The applause grows louder and louder.

10.   The program is successful.

Write It!   Imagine that you are at a Black History Month event. What is your favorite part? Write a description, using some predicate adjectives. Read your description to a friend.

Adjectives That Compare with ER and More

> • Add *er* to most adjectives to compare two nouns or pronouns.

With some adjectives of two or more syllables, use *more*. What you write to compare, remember these rules.

With adjectives that end with *e*, drop the final e and add *er*.
pure, purer   bare, barer   true, truer

If an adjective ends with a consonant and *y*, change the *y* to *i* and add *er*.
funny, funnier   happy, happier   lazy, lazier

If an adjective of one syllable ends with a single vowel and a consonant, double the final consonant and add *er*. Sad/sadder   hot/hotter

My sister is *sweeter* than a daisy. She seems *more sensitive* than my little cousin.

Try It!   Complete each sentence with the correct comparative form of the adjective in parentheses.

1.   My baby girl is (cute) than a button.   _____

2.   She is (intelligent) than her age suggests sometimes.   _____

3.   My mom says she acts (smart) than I did.   _____

4.   She certainly is (funny) than me.   _____

5.   Her first steps were (shaky) than a nervous hand.   _____

6.   She is (careful) now than she was a month ago.   _____

7.   Some of her faces are (silly) than a clown's.   _____

8.   Her smiles are (bright) than the sunshine.   _____

9.   Her belly is (big) than her head.   _____

10.   Her skin is (soft) than mine, because of the shea butter.   _____

Write It!   Is there a person or animal that you adore? Write a portrait of this person or animal. Use some adjectives that compare.

Adjectives That Compare with EST and Most

> • Add *est* to some adjectives to compare more than two nouns or pronouns.

With other adjectives of two or more syllables, use *most* to compare more than two nouns.

Never use *most* with the *est* form of an adjective. For more rules on forming comparisons with adjectives, see the lesson Adjectives That Compare with *er* and *More*.

I had the most amazing dream last night. In my dream, the wisest elder visited me.

Try It!   Rewrite each sentence, using the correct comparative form of the adjective in parentheses.

1.   Last night, I had the (incredible) dream.   _____

2.   Some of the (interesting) things happened.   _____

3.   The (great) leader of our people granted me three wishes. _____

4.   Of the three, my last wish was the (revolutionary).   _____

5.   I asked for the (wise) book in the world.   _____

6.   The book had the (amazing) affect of freeing all Black people from mental

slavery.   _____

7.   When I awoke, I was the (happy) person alive.   _____

8.   In my dream, I freed the (enslaved) people.   _____

9.   I taught them the (valuable) history about their culture. _____

10.   It was the (satisfying) dream I've ever had.   _____

Write It!   What's in a dream? Write a short story based on a dream you've had, or would like to have. You can be the most of anything or anybody. Read your story to someone in your family.

What Is an Adverb?

> • An **adverb** is a word that describes a verb. Adverbs tell *how, where,* or *when* an action took place. Many adverbs end in *ly.*

When you write about an action, you want to give your reader precise information about what occurred. Using adverbs is the way to do that. Look at these common adverbs.

How: together   happily   hard   eagerly   quickly   gently   softly
Where: under   inside   behind   here   forward   nearby   above
When: then   today   seldom   always   often   next   finally   last

Try It!   Draw a line under the adverb in each sentence. Draw two lines under the verb the adverb describes.

1.   We finally reached the maroon camp.

2.   I quickly made way to my aunt.

3.   Then I went to see my older cousin who had been there for two months.

4.   My uncle and brother came together to meet me.

5.   I always longed to reunite with them outside the plantation.

6.   I could hear small birds sing nearby.

7.   My cousin gently kissed me and welcomed me to freedom.

8.   The words swept softly across my body.

9.   Fluffy clouds floated above.

10.   We sung happily until nightfall.

Write It!   The first moments in a new place are often thrilling. Can you remember how it felt to arrive somewhere special? Write a journal entry about that time. Use many adverbs.

Adverbs That Tell How

> - An **adverb** can describe the action expressed by verb.
>   Adverbs that tell *how* can show *how much, with whom,*
>   and *in what way* an action happens.

Adverbs fine-tune verbs, giving a clearer picture of an action. Use them in sentences to add precision and clarity to your writing.

The fire in the village began *slowly*.
The griot *calmly* began his story.
A Queen Mother called *casually* to the watoto to sit.

Try It!   Complete each sentence with an adverb that tells how the action happens.

1.   The news _____spread throughout the organization.

2.   Two members _____planned the escape.

3.   The leader _____telephoned another member.

4.   He ordered that the operation begin _____.

5.   The warriors _____grabbed their guns and departed the house.

6.   The prison guards _____reacted to odd movement on the

grounds.

7.   The warden _____gave commands to fire.

8.   Assata _____grabbed her things.

9.   The Black Liberation Army _____fought as they fled to their car.

10.   Luckily, everyone had escaped _____and Assata was free.

Write It!   Have you ever been in a situation that called for brave action? Write a news article about this event. Use adverbs that tell how things happened.

Adverbs That Tell When

> • An **adverb** can tell *when* an action takes place.

Adverbs that tell when something happens give order and a clear sequence to your writing. You will notice that many of the adverbs tat tell when do not end in ly. Below are some adverbs that tell when about an action.

soon   always   often   today   finally   daily   sometimes
seldom   then   no   yesterday   tomorrow

Kwame *often* writes to his mother.

She *always* answers Kwame's letters with gifts.

Yesterday, his mother sent him a beautiful ankh necklace.

Try It!   Draw two lines under the adverb that describes each underlined verb.

1.   Today, few young people <u>know</u> of Stephen Biko.

2.   Biko <u>fought</u> daily to free Black people from apartheid in South Africa.

3.   Biko always <u>wrote</u> what he liked.

4.   And often <u>faced</u> criticism for his radical beliefs.

5.   He always <u>studied</u> hard.

6.   Soon he would <u>found</u> the South African Students' Organization to fight apartheid.

7.   He <u>wrote</u> articles on Black consciousness often.

8.   Biko <u>was</u> sometimes considered a terrorist.

9.   Then he <u>was taken</u> prisoner in August of 1977.

10.   Now, we <u>honor</u> Stephen Biko as one of our greatest warriors.

Write It!   What would you fight for? Family? A cause? Write a letter to a friend, explaining to them what you would fight for and why.

Adverbs That Tell Where

> • An **adverb** can tell *where* an action takes place.

In your writing, you can show the scene of the action by using adverbs that tell where events unfold. Below are some adverbs that tell *where*.

outside   inside   forward   backward   ahead   below
above   nearby   here   there

It was still dark *inside.*

The moon lingered *above.*

Try It!   Draw two lines under the adverb that describes each underlined verb.

1.   Ella Baker <u>was born</u> here in Norfolk, Virginia on December 13, 1903.

2.   She <u>went</u> to Shaw University in nearby North Carolina.

3.   Baker's style of leadership <u>was</u> outside of the norm.

4.   She did not think leaders should <u>sit</u> above their followers.

5.   Ella did not believe leaders should <u>exist</u> below either.

6.   She <u>wanted</u> to move the movement forward.

7.   Baker <u>desired</u> local leadership inside Black organizations.

8.   When the student sit-ins began, she <u>jumped</u> ahead and planned a conference.

9.   S.N.C.C. <u>developed</u> there in Raleigh, North Carolina.

10.   She stood strong on her convictions and never <u>looked</u> backward.

Write It!   Write a narrative about a special event or moment in your life. Be sure to use adverbs that tell where these events took place.

Adverbs That Compare with ER and More

> • **Adverbs** can compare actions.

When you write to compare two actions, you use comparative adverbs. Notice how these adverbs are formed.

The voice of wisdom grew *louder* than   the crashing thunder.
The lightning flashed more *brilliantly* than before.

Try It!   Complete each sentence with the correct comparative form of the adverb in parentheses.

1.   We forgot ourstory (quick) than our ancestors would have expected.

        _____

2.   The ignorance grew (hard) to deal with.   _____

3.   Some screamed the truth (loud) than before.   _____

4.   Yet, many seemed (desperate) than ever to get away from themselves.

        _____

5.   The music became (degrade) than mistrial shows.   _____

6.   The images portrayed us as (silly) than ever.   _____

7.   Some authors pushed knowledge (deep) than the deepest well.

        _____

8.   Certain singers sung ourstory (powerful) than the drums of Africa.

        _____

9.   The movement is growing (slow) than wanted, but it's moving.

        _____

10.   Fighting for our freedom is (urgent) than ever.   _____

Write It!   Reflect on some of our great leaders of yesterday. How do you think they would feel about our present position? Would they be proud? Use comparative adverbs to point up differences.

What is a Pronoun?

> • A **pronoun** is a word that takes the place of a noun.

Using pronouns when you write is a good way to avoid repeating a noun or group of words containing a noun. There are **subject pronouns** and **object pronouns**.
Subject Pronouns: I, you, he/she/it, we, you, they
Object Pronouns: me, you, him/her/it, us, you, them

The *song* is very long. *It* is at least seven minutes.
Buy directly from the *artist*. *She* receives more of the money that way.

Try It!   Replace each underlined word or group of words with a pronoun.

1.   <u>Bob Marley</u> sung freedom songs.   _____

2.   <u>Bob and the Wailers</u> recorded many albums.   _____

3.   <u>Benta and I</u> love his song called, "Zimbabwe."   _____

4.   <u>Bob Marley</u> practiced Rastafarianism.   _____

5.   Marley made songs with <u>Peter Tosh</u>.   _____

6.   Bob said, "Rita, I wrote this song for <u>Rita</u>."   _____

7.   My uncle found an album and gave it to <u>Densu</u>.   _____

8.   <u>Densu</u> was too young to really appreciate the music.   _____

9.   <u>Shiheem and Ky</u> enjoy his music though.   _____

10.   When they said Marley died of cancer, I couldn't believe <u>Tosin and Sankara</u>.

                                                                                         _____

Write It!   Listen to some Bob Marley songs. Which is your favorite? Write an extra verse to that song. Sing it to your family.

Subject Pronouns

> • A **subject pronoun** takes the place of a noun that is the subject of a sentence.

Subject pronouns are used after forms of the linking verb *be*. Use subject pronouns in your writing in order to avoid repeating the noun that is the sentence's subject. The subject pronouns are *I, you, he, she, it, we,* and *they*.

Delany practices his speech several times. *He* uses note cards as memory aids.

The speech concerns the liberation of Afrikan people. *It* is a great speech.

Try It!   Write each sentence, using a subject pronoun in place of the underlined word or words.

1.   <u>The warrior scholars</u> listened intently to Amilcar Cabral's speech.   _____

2.   <u>Cabral</u> is a persuasive speaker.   _____

3.   <u>The speech</u> asks the scholars to study Afrikan culture deeply.   _____

4.   <u>Language, philosophy, and clothes</u> are all apart of culture.   _____

5.   <u>Mwalimu Akoto</u> had a question about culture's role in revolution.   _____

6.   <u>Ifetayo and I</u> have some questions about Afrikan languages.   _____

7.   <u>Other scholars</u> also raised questions about cultural education.   _____

8.   <u>Our school</u> has many of Cabral speeches.   _____

9.   <u>All of us scholars</u> have our favorite Cabral quotes.   _____

10.   <u>Cabral's remarks</u> remind us of our responsibilities to our ancestors, our children, and the unborn.   _____

Write It!   How is our culture neglected? Write a persuasive speech about this topic. Use some subject pronouns in your writing. Read your speech to a group of your classmates or friends.

Object Pronouns

> - An **object pronoun** is a pronoun that can be used as the object of a verb or after words such as *to, with, for, at, with,* and *in.*

Using object pronouns in your writing helps you avoid repeating nouns needlessly. The object pronouns are *me, you, her, him, it, us,* and *them.*

Your new Afrikan dress is perfect on *you.* It would be impossible for *me* to sew that well. Mom still helps *us* with the hardest parts.

Try It!   Draw a line under the object pronoun in each sentence.

1.   Our mother teaches us how to sew.

2.   We've learned quite a bit from her.

3.   I will give some excellent tips to you.

4.   Some of the steps are difficult for me, but we must learn to make our own clothes.

5.   My baba is impressed by us.

6.   We made him a dashiki for Kwanzaa last year.

7.   Medgar and I bought some Afrikan fabric for it.

8.   The next project is an Ankara dress for each of my sisters.

9.   Jahzara cut out the cloth for them.

10.   Let me show you how beautiful we look in Afrikan clothing.

Write It!   Are you working on a special project? Write a paragraph about something you are learning to do or make. Read over your paragraph and check for the correct use of object pronouns.

Using I and ME

> • Use *I* as the subject of a sentence or after the linking verb *be*. Use *me* after action verbs or after a word such as *in, at, to, for,* or *with*.

A compound subject can contain *I*, or a compound object can contain *me*. To figure out which one to use, leave out the other word in the compound.

The use of the subject pronoun *I* and the object pronoun *me* can be confusing. Get them straight in your writing by remembering the rules.

You and *I* enjoy fufu. *I* enjoy fufu.
The drums are perfect for Najji and *me*. The drums are perfect for *me*.

Try It!   Complete each sentence correctly, using *I* or *me*.

1.   _____ love Ghana.

2.   The sunny weather seems ideal to _____.

3.   You and _____ enjoyed our time there last summer.

4.   Mama Ama had many lessons for Kwame and _____.

5.   Mama Adwoa had lessons for you and _____, too.

6.   Fugar and _____ spoke Twi to the natives.

7.   He told _____ how to greet others in the language.

8.   You and _____ went to an Okomfo.

9.   She did a reading for you and _____.

10.   Give _____ Ghana any day.

Write It!   Have you are been to a country in Africa? If not, which would you like to visit. Why? If you have, write a paragraph about what you enjoyed most on your trip. You are writing about yourself, so use I and me.

Using We and Us

> • The **subject pronoun** we can be used with a noun or after forms of the verb be. The **object pronoun** us can be used after action verbs or after words such as *for, at, with,* and *to.*

You can use we and us with nouns to make your writing clear. Look at the examples below.

The protest was exciting to *us* students.

We pupils thoroughly enjoyed the experience.

Try It!   Underline the correct word from each pair in parentheses.

1.   (We, Us) visitors obeyed the posted rules at the Elmina Slave Dungeon.

2.   A tour guide explained the rules to (we, us).

3.   No one complained about the tour but (we, us).

4.   (We, Us) lovers of African people could not listen to lies.

5.   Professor Nkrumah said he would give (we, us) the true history.

6.   (We, Us) took pictures of everything.

7.   (We, Us) poured libation to our ancestors.

8.   We could feel their spirits around (we, us).

9.   The smells brought (we, us) back.

10.   (We, Us) will never forget that experience.

Write It!   When was the last time you went somewhere and felt very strong emotions? Write a letter to a friend about the experience. Use we and us to make your meaning clear.

Possessive Pronouns Before Nouns

> • **Possessive pronouns** show ownership. They show who
> or what owns something. The possessive pronouns *my,
> your, his, her, its, our,* and *their* are used before nouns.

You can use possessive pronouns in your writing to show ownership of one or more
persons, places, or things. Never use an apostrophe (') with a possessive pronoun.

Sojourner Truth's work was impressive. *Her* work concerned Black rights.

The museum contains her pictures. *Its* collection is informative.

Try It!   Rewrite each sentence using a possessive pronoun instead of the
underlined word or words.

1.   Miles Davis' music was revolutionary.

2.   The trumpet's sound was warm and electric.

3.   The band's innovation never stopped.

4.   The jazz players' technical mastery was unrivalled.

5.   Charles Parker's help was useful to Miles Davis.

6.   The tunes belonging to Miles changed the game.

7.   Imhotep and my special interest is Bebop jazz.

8.   The club's manager paid these musicians well.

9.   How good is the music school you attend?

10.   What do you think of the Miles Davis project that I will do?

Write It!   Choose a famous Black musician and write a paragraph about what
they added to their musical genre.

Possessive Pronouns Alone

> • **Possessive pronouns** stand alone when they take the place of a noun in a sentence. The possessive pronouns *mine, yours, his, hers, its, ours,* and *theirs* can stand alone.

A possessive pronoun is a pronoun that shows who or what owns something. You can vary your sentences by replacing some nouns with possessive pronouns.

That is my costume. That costume is *mine.*

Your costume is still in the trunk. *Yours* is still in the trunk.

Try It!   Replace the underlined word or words with the correct possessive pronoun that stands alone.

1.   The best monologue is <u>the one belonging to him</u>.   _____

2.   <u>Your part</u> is most important.   _____

3.   <u>Their lines</u> are directed towards Mr. Younger.   _____

4.   <u>Its theme</u> is the clash between dreams and poverty.   _____

5.   <u>My costume</u> is from the Africa. I'm Beneatha Younger.   _____

6.   <u>Our mother</u> is a strong woman.   _____

7.   <u>Her talent</u> is keeping a family to together.   _____

8.   What is <u>your favorite part of the play</u>?   _____

9.   <u>My favorite</u> is when they finally move out.   _____

10.   <u>That family's problems</u> are still here.   _____

Write It!   Imagine you are writing a play. What would be the theme or main idea of the play? Write out the main plot of the play. Include some possessive pronouns that can stand-alone.

Verb Agreement with Pronouns

> • A verb must agree with the pronoun that is the subject of the sentence.

When your sentence includes a pronoun as its subject, the subject pronoun and the verb must agree. A singular pronoun takes a singular verb. A plural pronoun takes a plural verb.

I <u>take</u> a bus to school. *It* <u>picks</u> me up at seven-thirty in the morning.

You <u>walk</u> to school with your older brothers. *They* <u>look</u> after you.

Try It!   In each sentence, underline the correct verb from the pair in parentheses.

1.   I frequently (study, studies) the writing of Amos Wilson.

2.   You (read, reads) the work of Frances Cress Welsing.

3.   We sometimes (go, goes) to the library to study together.

4.   They (is, are) our favorite scholars.

5.   It (take, takes) me only a few days to read a book by one of them.

6.   I rarely (watch, watches) reality television.

7.   She (sleep, sleeps) with books.

8.   It (make, makes) her happy to have wisdom always there.

9.   We (teach, teaches) each other what we learn.

10.   They (help, helps) decolonize our minds.

Write It!   Do you love books? If not, why? Write a paragraph about your relationship with books. Why do you like or dislike them?

What is a Preposition?

> • A **preposition** is a word that relates a noun or pronoun to another word in a sentence. The **object of a preposition** is the noun or pronoun that follows the preposition.

Using prepositions in your writing is the way to show relationships between other words. Choose the preposition that makes the relationship clear.

I love to visit *with* Grandpa and Grandma. They are so good *to* me.

Here are some often-used prepositions.
about   after   along   among   around   at   by   during   except   for
from   in   into   of   on   over   past   through   to   until   with   without.

Try It!   Draw one line under each preposition. Draw two lines under the object of each preposition.

1.   Langston Hughes wrote from the heart.

2.   One poem was about rivers.

3.   "I've Known Rivers" takes the reader through the history of African people.

4.   Jazz poetry lived inside his mind.

5.   He wrote short stories until late in life.

6.   His characters spoke with great power and wit.

7.   You should learn about Langston Hughes.

8.   He produced great work during the Harlem Renaissance.

9.   Hughes was from Joplin, Missouri.

10.   He stands among the great writers of all time.

Write It!   Read Langston Hughes poem, "I've Known Rivers" and draw an illustration that describes the poem. Show it to your parents.

The Object of a Preposition

> • The **object of a preposition** is the noun or pronoun that follows the preposition. When the object of a preposition is a pronoun, use an **object pronoun**.

When your writing contains a compound object that includes a pronoun, check the pronoun by leaving out the other object in the compound. The object pronouns are *me, you, him, her, it, us,* and *them.*

Mr. Armah gave his old tools to Maat and me.
Mr. Armah gave his old tools to me.

The tools were given to children.
They immediately showed them to Baba.

Try It!   Draw a line under the object of each preposition in the sentence.

1.   That African proverb book was the best present for Makena.

2.   My sister sat right down with it.

3.   She wrote stories about the proverbs.

4.   She found a friend to go over them with her.

5.   Obi received a shield from Grandpa.

6.   He became a warrior without a second thought.

7.   They forgot their surroundings for a moment.

8.   Brother warrior and sister prophet played until bedtime.

9.   Baba even studied the proverbs during the night.

10.   Their presence brought good energy to our home.

Write It!   Write a paragraph on your thoughts about this African proverb:
Bravery at home is no bravery at all.

Prepositional Phrases

> • A **prepositional phrase** is a group of words that begins with a preposition and ends with a noun or pronoun.

In your sentences, a prepositional phrase can come at the beginning, middle, or end of a sentence. Place it as close as possible to the word or words to which it relates.

The new community center has excellent resources *in it*.
The gym instructor, *with our classroom teacher*, unveiled new exercises.
For an hour, we worked our muscles.

Try It!   Draw one line under each prepositional phrase. Draw two lines under each object of a preposition.

1.   In 1966, Stokely Carmichael became chairman of S.N.C.C..

2.   As a student at Howard University, he started his activist career.

3.   Malcolm X influenced him greatly in the 1960s.

4.   Carmichael worked in Lowndes County, Alabama to increase Black voting.

5.   He was apart of the Black Panther Party for awhile.

6.   To honor Kwame Nkrumah and Sekou Ture, Stokely changed his name to Kwame Ture.

7.   From the late 1970s until his death, he answered the phone: "Ready for Revolution."

8.   During his time in Guinea, Ture published a book called *Stokely Speaks*.

9.   Ture filled his life with revolutionary love.

10.   During his life, Kwame Ture inspired us to fight for Black Power.

Write It!   Ture changed his name from a European name. Do you think African people should go by European names? Write a paragraph answering this question.

End Punctuation

> • **End punctuation** marks the end of a sentence. The three types of end punctuation are a **period**, a **question mark**, and an **exclamation mark**.

In your writing, you use a period (.) to end a statement or a command. You use a question mark (?) to end a question. You use an exclamation mark (!) to end an exclamation.

Come and watch this documentary on the Nation of Islam.
Do you know who you are?
Black man is god and the Black woman is goddess!

Try It!   Complete each sentence by adding the correct end punctuation mark.

1.   Elijah Muhammad was the leader of the Nation of Islam

2.   Study his philosophy

3.   Do you know one of his best students

4.   The Nation of Islam stressed self-sufficiency

5.   Are we too dependent on other groups

6.   Yes, it is time to fix that

7.   Muhammad had only a third grade education

8.   MGT classes help build strong women

9.   Have you read *Message to the Black Man*

10.   Know thyself

Write It!   Research how the Nation of Islam promoted self-sufficiency. What practical skills will you develop to help your community. Write a letter to your parents to inform them of your plans.

Commas

> • A **comma (,)** is used to set off or separate words or phrases in a sentence.

Commas are also used between the names of cities and states and between the day and the year in dates. Commas can separate words in a series and set off an appositive. Use them to keep your writing clear.

Commas Between Place Names and Numbers: Oakland, California August 17, 1887
Commas in a Series: We need butter, eggs, and flour.
Commas After Words and Phrases: Yes, I will shop for them today.
Commas to Set Off an Appositive: Toussaint, a warrior, fought hard.

Try It!   To each sentence, add commas where they are needed.

1.   On August 28 1955 Emmett Till was lynched.

2.   The lynching took place in Money Mississippi.

3.   Till only 14 at the time was visiting from Chicago.

4.   He was a happy funny and sweet person to be around.

5.   Yes he bragged sometimes.

6.   After reportedly flirting with a white woman white men took him from his home.

7.   The woman was 21 years old white and named Carolyn.

8.   The men beat gouged out one of his eyes and shoot Emmett.

9.   After the trial the white men bragged about how they killed him.

10.   Till's body was shipped back to Chicago Illinois.

Write It!   Look online for pictures of Emmett Till. Write a paragraph on your thoughts about what happened to him.

Colons

> • A **colon** can be used to separate two main clauses. A colon can also set off a list or series. A colon can be used to separate hours and minutes in time. A colon follows the greeting of a business letter.

Colon Between Clauses: We cannot forget the lesson of the Haitian Revolution: committed fighters can win.
Colon Setting Off a List or Series: We study the greats: Marcus, Malcolm, Mandela
Colon to Show Time: 4:33
Colon After Greeting: Dear Mwalimu:

Try It!   Use a colon to punctuate each sentence.

1.   At 10 30, we have an Ourstory test.

2.   The exam will require hard work it is all essay questions.

3.   We will write about three things Ancient Ghana, Mali, and Songhai.

4.   My essay could be in the form of a letter beginning "Dear Asantehene."

5.   I know a lot about the following Sundiata Keita, Mansa Musa, and Sonni Ali.

6.   I will write about two factors Islam and trade.

7.   Our class now knows which kingdoms were most powerful in West Africa.

8.   At 11 30, the exam papers will be collected.

9.   Mwalimu Baruti has three tasks to real all papers, to grade them, and to return them.

10.   The unit will be over, but not finished we will never forget these lessons.

Write It!   What era of African history fascinates you? Write a brief report outlining some key facts about this period. Did you use colons where they are needed? Read your report to a group of your friends.

Quotation Marks

> • **Quotation marks** are used before and after a direct quotation. Use quotation marks to set off the titles of poems, songs, short stories, articles, and book chapters.

In your writing, use quotation marks (" ") to show a speaker's exact words. Set off direct quotations with either a comma or a colon.

"I enjoy reading poetry," Bookman said. He mentioned one of his favorite poems: "Somebody Blew Up America" by Amiri Baraka.

Try It!   Add quotation marks and proper punctuation to each group of words that is either a direct quotation or the title of a literary work.

1.   Reading makes me think remarked Chike.

2.   Last night, I read the selection African Will Rise.

3.   Yes, that is a good poem commented Mama Akua.

4.   It tells the beginning of our revolution Femi added.

5.   Today we will read a story about another famous African said Mama Akua.

6.   We opened our books to Biko's Story.

7.   This story inspired me, Ngozi admitted.

8.   Last week's literature assignment was Dead Men's Path.

9.   Our theme for this unit is African Literature Mama Akua reminded us.

10.   We also read the chapter titled Roots of Revolution.

Write It!   Imagine that you are discussing a reading assignment with a group of classmates. Use quotation marks to show exactly what each person says. Be sure to use quotation marks to set off the titles of stories, poems, or songs.

Italics and Underlining

> - Use *italics* for the titles of publications, movies, works of art, television and radio programs, and musical recordings. You can also <u>underline</u> these titles when you type or write by hand. Use *italics* to set off letters of the alphabet, words, foreign words, and numbers used as words.

The Journal of Black History or <u>The Journal of Black History</u>
The word *asante* comes to us from East Africa.

Try It!   Underline the title in each sentence. Write *italics* if a sentence contains a word that should be italicized.

1.   The Negro World published articles on current events and issues important

to African people.   _____

2.   The Louisiana Weekly covered two jazz concerts yesterday. _____

3.   Have you heard that album, Mama Africa?   _____

4.   Yes, I'm a great aficionado of reggae music.   _____

5.   What famous reggae band begins with the letter w?   _____

6.   The word wailer appears in its name.   _____

7.   I read about the band's legacy in Essence magazine.   _____

8.   Did you see Bob Marley on Good Morning, Africa?   _____

9.   Yes, he sang his song, Zimbabwe.   _____

10.   Did you ever see the movie Marley?   _____

Write It!   With friends, do you ever discuss movies or songs? Write a script in which you and your friends talk over some of your favorite entertainments.

Apostrophes

> • An **apostrophe** is used in a contraction to show where letters have been left out. An apostrophe is used with nouns to show possession.

To show possession, add 's to singular nouns and to plural nouns that do not end in *s*. You add an apostrophe (') alone to plural nouns that do end in *s*.

Use apostrophes when your writing contains contractions and possessive nouns.
It**'s** too bad you were sick yesterday. I went to Nneka*'s* concert by myself.
The musicians' talent was inspiring. The audience*'s* applause was sincere.

Try It!   Add an apostrophe to each contraction or possessive noun.

1.   The writers style was intriguing.

2.   Ive never been so fascinated in my life.

3.   Were going to attend the next play together, okay?

4.   Angolas Warriors are performing in December.

5.   A singers voice is his musical instrument.

6.   Its a wonderful ability, isnt it?

7.   Youll want more tickets next year.

8.   Theyll feature the greatest African dancers.

9.   Last year, my aunt invited her womens club.

10.   Everyone loved the groups passion and talent.

Write It!   Describe the best concert or performance you have ever attended. Check for the correct use of apostrophes in your writing.

Abbreviations

> - An **abbreviation** is the shortened form of a word.

You can abbreviate, or shorten, certain words in addresses, titles, and lists. Initials are one type of abbreviation. Time can also be abbreviated: A.M. means before noon; P.M. means after noon. Be sure to check that you have used the correct abbreviations in your writing. Notice how some words are abbreviated in the heading and address of the letter below.

Dr. Samori S. Camara
1925 RBG Ave.
Little Afrika, LA 70114

Try It!   Write the correct abbreviation for each underlined word below.

1.   Their house was the green one on Freedman <u>Avenue</u>.   _____

2.   <u>Mister</u> Imani's store is on the corner.   _____

3.   Turn right onto Uhuru <u>Street</u>.   _____

4.   The meeting is on <u>August the seventh</u>.   _____

5.   It will begin at four o'clock <u>in the afternoon</u>.   _____

6.   I left a flyer at your <u>apartment</u>.   _____

7.   Our aunt is coming all the way from <u>Alabama</u>.   _____

8.   Her name is Fannie <u>Lou</u> Hamer.   _____

9.   She is the owner of Kamali Marketplace and <u>Company</u>.   _____

10.   If you want to ride with her, meet her at Nguvu <u>Street</u>.   _____

Write It!   Write an invitation to a meeting about Black Business ownership. Be sure to include names, titles, and addresses on your flyer.

Parentheses

> • **Parentheses ( )** are used to set off information that is not needed in order to understand the main idea of a sentence.

Much like commas, parentheses show the relationship between the different parts of a sentence. In your writing, use parentheses around groups of words that are of less importance than the rest of the sentence.

Malcolm (one of six children) became a revolutionary.

Nzinga (a strong queen) led her people into battle.

Try It!   Place parentheses around the part of each sentence that seems less important than the rest of the sentence.

1.   The national convention held in Gary, Indiana explored the goals of Black Power.

2.   The participants many of them Black Nationalists gathered to exchange ideas.

3.   Some of the popular ideas just to mention a few included community control of schools, Black political power, and national health care.

4.   Amiri Baraka a poet and activist led the proceedings.

5.   Thousands of Black people from across the country attended this important event.

6.   All those who attended the convention which lasted three days said they benefited from the experience.

7.   The members who were excited shouted, "It's Nation Time."

8.   Some delegates who wanted to focus on integration protested the resolutions for Black schools.

9.   Young and older people and there were plenty of each group all had an educational experience.

10.   The convention which was a powerful statement should happen again annually.

Write It!   Should Black people have their own schools? Why or why not? In a paragraph, explain your answer. See if there is any information, which should be in parentheses.

Synonyms

> • A **synonym** is a word that has the same or nearly the same meaning as another word. A word may have more than one synonym.

When several words have almost the same definition, you choose the one that best fits your meaning. If you are unsure which word to use in your writing, you can check a dictionary or a thesaurus.

Marva Collins was a *wonderful* teacher. Claud Anderson is a *marvelous* teacher.

His muscles are *powerful*. His muscles are *strong*.

Try It!   Rewrite each sentence, replacing the underlined word with a synonym.

1.   The Berlin Conference <u>harmed</u> Africa.   _____

2.   It <u>happened</u> in 1884.   _____

3.   No African nations were <u>present</u> at the conference.   _____

4.   Europeans <u>divided</u> Africa among themselves.   _____

5.   The goal was to steal African resources to <u>enrich</u> their countries.

                    _____

6.   This <u>time period</u> is called the Scramble for Africa.   _____

7.   Millions died <u>horrible</u> deaths at the hands of these invaders.

                    _____

8.   This event <u>started</u> European colonization of Africa, which continues today.

                    _____

9.   Many Africans fought <u>hard</u> against the invasion.   _____

10.   Physical and mental <u>colonization</u> must end.   _____

Write It!   Lookup the Berlin Conference. In a paragraph, discuss how it affected the African continent.

Antonyms

> • **Antonyms** are words with opposite meanings.

A word may have more than one antonym. In your writing, choose an antonym when you want to contrast two things or qualities. Notice that the word serious has several antonyms, each slightly different in meaning.

Kali is *serious*. Amina is *lighthearted*. Amina is *giddy*.

Try It!   Fill in the blank with an antonym for the underlined word.

1.   Claud Anderson is my most <u>knowledgeable</u> friend.   _____

2.   Obenga was the <u>best</u> student of Diop.   _____

3.   Sertima is always <u>early</u> with the information.   _____

4.   Kambon earns <u>many</u> awards for his courage.   _____

5.   Essex was <u>confident</u> before the rebellion.   _____

6.   My <u>strongest</u> subject is mental math.   _____

7.   The teacher <u>encourages</u> me all the time.   _____

8.   Delany exercises <u>enthusiastically</u> in gym class.   _____

9.   Asantewaa <u>often</u> volunteers to help others.   _____

10.   Nzinga is <u>disturbed</u> by the lack of African pride.   _____

Write It!   What is life in your classroom like? Write a comparison-contrast paragraph about the different personalities of your classmates.

Homographs

> • **Homographs** are words that are spelled the same but that have different meanings. Homographs may also be pronounced differently.

Writers find that there are a number of words that have the same spellings, but that have quite different definitions. In that case, you should consider the context, or overall meaning, of the sentence in which the word is used.

I am shopping for Kwanzaa *presents*. Every year, our family *presents* educational gifts to one another.

I *saw* a good set of tools at the hardware store. There was a great *saw* for Baba.

Try It!   Write the correct definition of the underlined homograph.

1.   Griots have a <u>record</u> of ourstory in their heads.   _____

2.   You don't look at a <u>watch</u> when they speak.   _____

3.   Just <u>close</u> your eyes and listen intently.   _____

4.   I sat to the <u>right</u> of him.   _____

5.   Others <u>watch</u> from a distance.   _____

6.   As he spoke, a <u>dove</u> flew overhead.   _____

7.   His <u>pipe</u> bellowed with smoke.   _____

8.   After the story, we all drank from the same <u>pitcher</u>.   _____

9.   It felt <u>fine</u> to learn my story.   _____

10.   The <u>spirit</u> of his message lingers today.   _____

Write It!   A griot is also known as a djeli. Djeli means "blood." How is knowing ourstory like the blood in our bodies?

Homophones

> - **Homophones** are words that sound alike but have different meanings and spellings. Consider the context of your sentence to determine which spelling is right.

Homophones can be tricky. In your writing, be sure to choose the homophone that fits your meaning. Compare the two pairs of sentences below.

I walked *by* the Black grocery store. I needed to *buy* some ingredients.
The store had a *red* open sign. I *read* the store hours on the sign.

Try It!   Underline the correct homophone from each pair in parentheses.

1.   The vegetarian recipe calls for (flour, flower), sugar, butter, and spices.

2.   I remembered to (right, write) the ingredients on my list.

3.   Baba (scent, sent) me to get what we needed.

4.   I (know, no) how to choose the best ingredients.

5.   The spices are (hear, here) on the table.

6.   We need more vegetables, (to, too, two).

7.   At (night, knight) we will make fufu.

8.   I will (wear, where, ware) my new kente cloth apron.

9.   Juma can use my old (blew, blue) one.

10.   We will make the (dough, doe) for our Kwanzaa treats.

Write It!   Imagine you are preparing a dish for a Kwanzaa Karamu. What would you make? What ingredients and special preparation would be necessary? Write a set of directions or a recipe for this dish.

Name: Date:

Context Clues

> • **Context clues** are words that you already know. These words help you to figure out the meaning of unfamiliar words in a sentence.

Some words in your writing may be new to your reader. If you think a word in one of your sentences needs explanation, give your reader some clues. These known words give the context, or setting, of the new word.

The singer had a remarkable *range*, covering high and low notes smoothly.

In the sentence above, the words *high* and *low* are the clues that help readers guess the definition of the word *range*.

Try It!   Using context clues, write a definition of the underlined word on a separate sheet of paper.

1.   The singer's high, clear <u>soprano</u> rang through the concert hall.
2.   Never flat or sharp, she had perfect <u>pitch</u>.
3.   Her <u>accompanist</u>, a perfect partner for her, played the piano beautifully.
4.   The performers got several <u>encores</u>, and graciously offered another song after each round of applause.
5.   The <u>program</u>, which included many beloved songs, was a truly excellent presentation.
6.   Although we had seats high up in the <u>balcony</u> above the orchestra, we were able to see and hear quite well.
7.   The lovely singer was just back from a <u>triumphant</u> tour of Africa, in which she dazzled audiences and won great praise from all.
8.   I was so <u>enchanted</u> by the music's spell, I might have been in fairyland.
9.   Once outside of the concert hall, my peaceful mood was <u>shattered</u> by the honking of cars and the screech of sirens.
10.   The <u>tumult</u> around me, a sea of noise and flashing lights, put an end to my dreamy mood once and for all.

Write It!   Write a song about a magical moment.

Troublesome Words

> - **Troublesome words** are words that often confuse writers.

There are certain words in our language that are often misspelled or mistaken for other, similar-looking or –sounding words. Check your writing for these and other troublesome words. When you are unsure which to use, refer to a dictionary.

angel/angle clase/clothes lose/loose accept/except whether/weather
we're/were quiet/quite though/through your/you're relief/relieve
bought/brought.

Try It!   Underline the correct word from each pair in parentheses.

1.   Everyone wears African (clothes, close) for the event.

2.   (We're, Were) ready for revolution now.

3.   The (whether, weather) is sunny and warm.

4.   We'll walk (though, through) the movement together.

5.   (Your, You're) dressed perfectly for the journey.

6.   Our minds are (quite, quiet) while we meditate.

7.   The leader (brought, bought) mats for everyone.

8.   What a (relief, relieve) to be back on the road to tradition.

9.   We didn't (lose, loose) all of our African ways.

10.   North is the (angle, angel) we must take to freedom.

Write It!   Write an article about how we can practice Sankofa everyday.

Specific Nouns

> - **Specific nouns** name the individual members of a class or group of items. **General nouns** refer to any of a class or group.

When you want to be precise in your writing, use specific nouns. These nouns show exactly whom or what you mean.

General Nouns: horse   home   cat

Specific Nouns: Clydesdale   apartment   Siamese

Try It!   Rewrite each sentence, replacing the underlined general noun with a specific noun.

1.   My <u>home</u> has a red, black, and green flag on the wall.   _____

2.   I live in a <u>rural community</u>.   _____

3.   There are many large <u>trees</u> around the house.   _____

4.   I also have some great <u>pets</u>.   _____

5.   Baba built a beautiful <u>building</u> to house our harvested vegetables.

                                                                                                                     _____

6.   My mama grows <u>flowers</u> in her garden.   _____

7.   She also likes to sew <u>dresses</u>.   _____

8.   Her specialty is <u>shirts</u>.   _____

9.   My dada (sister) loves to take care of <u>animals</u>.   _____

10.   I prefer to read <u>books</u>.   _____

Write It!   Where would you like to live? Write a paragraph about that place. Use specific nouns that show precisely what your surroundings are like.

Prefixes

> • A **prefix** is a word part that is added to the beginning of a base word. A prefix changes the meaning of a base word.

You can expand your vocabulary by using prefixes in your writing. Study the following prefixes and their meanings.

re	again, back	un, dis	not, the opposite of
mis	wrong, wrongly	im, in	not, without, in, into
il, ir	not, without	non	not, the opposite of, without
pre	before, in preparation for	post	after, later

Try It!   Change the meaning of each underlined word by adding a prefix. Check to be sure that the rewritten sentence makes sense.

1.   The scholar <u>views</u> the ancient record.   _____

2.   She thinks the Kemetic arguments are <u>logical</u>.   _____

3.   Some ideas seem <u>possible</u>.   _____

4.   She decides to <u>arrange</u> the research into subjects.   _____

5.   That way, there will be less <u>sense</u> in the information. _____

6.   The student is im<u>pressed</u>, too.   _____

7.   He thinks our ancestors <u>presented</u> the facts well.   _____

8.   A parent, too, <u>learned</u> a lot.   _____

9.   The information was largely <u>known</u> before now.   _____

10.   We must <u>consider</u> who we are and where we come from. _____

Write It!   Is there an argument about African people that upsets you? Write an editorial on the subject. Use some prefixes in your writing.

Suffixes

> - A **suffix** is a word part added to the end of a base word.
>   A suffix changes the meaning of a base word.

You can add a suffix to a word to change its meaning or its part of speech. Look at the following suffixes and their definitions.

ful	full of	*able, ible*	capable
ness	state of being	*less*	without, that does not
ment	the act, quality of	*ation, ition*	state of being, result of
ward	in the direction of	*ly*	in a _____ way
er, or	one or something that __	*ist*	one who does or makes
an, ian	one who believes in, or comes from		
y	full of, somewhat, like		

Try It!   Change each underlined base word by adding the correct suffix.

1.   My kaka (brother) told me a <u>wonder</u> story.   _____

2.   I listened <u>careful</u> to the story about Nat Turner.   _____

3.   The lessons were quite <u>value</u>.   _____

4.   Turner fought to end the <u>enslave</u> of African people in Virginia.

     _____

5.   His <u>bold</u> still inspires us today.   _____

6.   He was a true <u>liberate</u>.   _____

7.   Turner demonstrated <u>eager</u> for freedom.   _____

8.   Nat Turner was a <u>fear</u> warrior.   _____

9.   I always look <u>for</u> to the stories of my kaka.   _____

10.   I become more <u>knowledge</u> whenever we see each other. _____

Write It!   Who tells the best stories in your family? Share one of their stories.